OLD TIMES

REMINISCENCES OF THE EARLY DAYS OF MICHIGAN.

An Address by

GOV. JOHN J. BAGLEY

before the

Cass County Pioneer Association,

WEDNESDAY, JUNE 21, 1876.

DETROIT:
Wm. Graham's Steam Presses, 52 Bates Street.
1876.

OLD TIMES.

REMINISCENCES OF THE EARLY DAYS OF MICHIGAN.

GOV. BAGLEY AT THE CASS COUNTY PIONEER PICNIC.

The pioneers of Cass County held a general festival and picnic at Cassopolis on Wednesday, the 21st, and among those who contributed to the reminiscences of the occasion was Gov. Bagley. He spoke as follows:

My Friends—If you had asked me to come here and talk of politics—if you had invited me to "make a speech," I should not have come, but when you said, "come and talk of old times and early days," I could not say no. We find in the dictionary that the verb pioneer means to go before—prepare the way for. The noun pioneer meant originally a foot soldier or foot passenger—one who goes before to remove obstructions or prepare the way for others. How fully we who have been pioneers appreciate and understand these technical definitions of the word, and yet how incomplete and imperfect they are! Foot passengers, indeed, we were. It was easier to walk than to ride, but whether it was or not, we walked. The few household goods we owned, the spinning wheel and the family oven, filled the wagon, and mother and the children chinked into the spare places, and we and the dog walked. Preparers of the way, indeed, were we. The roads we built, the log bridges we threw across the streams we did not destroy, but left for those who were to come after us. The pioneer was unselfish. He cared not whether friend or foe was behind him; if he could make his way any more easy, he was glad of it. He felt that he was in partnership with the world—"a fellow feeling made him wondrous kind." He was the advance guard of an army—countless in numbers, irresistible in its power—an army that knew no such word as fail and listened to no order for retreat.

The pioneer was the child of progress. He looked up, and not down; forward, and not back. Behind him was the past, before him the future. He felt that the wise men came from the East, and took courage. The needle of his compass always pointed westward, and he followed it.

Our pioneer dreamed dreams and saw visions. He dreamed of the old home on the hillside of New England or the quiet valleys of New York—of gray-haired father and mother, watching from the low door-way the departing children, or perchance sleeping in the village churchyard; perhaps of smaller green mounds covering his John or Kate—or of the country church, where theologic dust knocked from the pulpit cushion in the good old orthodox way, had so often closed his eyes and ears on drowsy Sunday afternoons—or of the spelling bee or singing school, where he first met the country lass

> "Who tying her bonnet under her chin,
> Had tied the young man's heart within,"

and kept it tied forever after His dreams were of the yesterdays—his visions were of to-morrow. He foresaw hard work and hard times, back-ache and heart-ache, blue days and weary nights, but he saw too in the dim future the town, the village, the city, the county, the State, an empire of itself—he saw thousands of homes and hundreds of thousands of owners, happy, prosperous people—he saw schools and churches, factories and fertile fields, institutions of science and learning—he saw capital and labor, brain and body, mind and muscle, all employed in the advancement of civilization, and the permanent improvement of mankind. And of all this he was to be a part and parcel. What visions were these! Do you wonder that the pioneer was a pioneer, brave, cheerful and faithful?

Though his visions were grand, the realization is grander still. He builded better than he knew, but with abundant faith in the future, adopted as the motto of the State "*Si queris peninsulam amœnam circumspice*," (if thou seekest a beautiful peninsula behold it here), and thanks to his strong right arm and courageous heart, we do behold it—covered with quiet villages, thriving cities, fruitful fields and blooming orchards, dotted all over with happy homes, with schools and colleges, churches and public institutions that tell the story of a civilization, grand in its conception, and mighty in its progress. This is the handiwork of the pioneer, the ripened crop of the white covered wagon.

We look back to the old times, as hard times, and so they were; full hearts and empty purses, hard work and plenty of it, shivering ague and wasting fever were the common lot of our early settlers, yet they had their share of good times too, and were free from many a plague that annoys their children.

Hard money and soft money were not debatable questions. You may remember the story of the man who, when he heard that the Bank of Constantine had failed said, "His heart came into his mouth when he heard of it, and he rushed home and to the bureau drawer, when he found he hadn't any Constantine money or any other sort." He was a pioneer.

Butter and eggs were pin-money; wheat paid the store-keeper; sled-length knotty wood that wouldn't make fence rails paid the minister, while an occasional pig or a grist of corn or wheat paid the doctor. Trade was the order of the day—the necessity of the time. And so we traded and dickered and swapped, exchanging products and helping one another; and while in the outside world bankers talked of stocks and values—politicians quarreled over tariffs and free trade, and statesmen wrote of the laws of trade, of corporations, monopolies, finance, etc., etc., somehow or other, in our trading and dickering we managed to grow a little better off from year to year.

Quarrelsome school meetings were unknown in those days. We never fought over the question of whether we should build a three story school-house with a basement or a four story one without, or whether we should put a cupola or a mortgage on it. We built our log school-house, set the teacher at work and boarded him round the neighborhood.

The religious life of the pioneer was free from sectarianism. The itinerant minister doing his Master's work was always welcome to home and hearth-stone. The school-house was open to him, regardless of his creed. He baptized and buried and married and asked no questions, and got but few fees.

The different schools of medicine let the pioneer kindly alone.

The boneset and wormwood, pennyroyal and catnip that hung on the chimney breast or the rafters in the roof were commonly enough; but if not, when we called in the hard-worked, poorly-paid, yet patient and jolly doctor, we did not question his "pathy" or his diploma. It may have been parchment or paper, from a college on earth, or in no man's-land, but we were sure his pills would be big enough, and that we could safely trust his jalap and cream of tarter, his calomel and quinine.

Questions of domestic economy and home discipline that do worry the best of us now-a-days gave the pioneer but little trouble. No dispute could be gotten up over the pattern of the parlor carpet, for they hadn't any—or if they had, it was of rags. The fashion plates did not reach the woods in those days, and Jane's bonnet and Charlie's coat were worn regardless of style till they were worn out, and then they were made over for the younger children. Who called first, and who called last, and who owed calls, were not debatable questions with our mothers; they visited when they had time and wanted to—and when they didn't they stayed at home.

Insurance agents did not worry the pioneer—his log house was fire proof. Patent-right peddlers haunted him not, for necessity made him his own inventor. Lightning-rod agents, smooth-tongued and oily, let him alone, as lightning had no terrors for him. The jaunty, affable sewing-machine man had not been born to trouble the souls of our mothers. Mellifluous melodeons were not set up in the parlor on trial. The robins and the frogs, the orioles and the owls made music enough for him.

The height and color, the architecture and structure of the first house gave us no uneasiness. It was built of logs any way.

If we were inclined to be extravagant we painted the door and window casings red, making the paint of buttermilk and brick dust. The pathway to the gate was lined with pinks and four-o'clocks, sweet williams and larkspur—(Latin names for American flowers had not been invented then.) Hollyhocks and sunflowers lifted their stately heads at either end of the house; morning-glorys climbed gracefully over the two front windows, and the hop vine, with its drooping bells, crept quietly over the door.

The patent pump, or rattling wind-mill were as yet unknown, the well-sweep lifted its awkward hand as if beckoning one to quench his thirst from "the old oaken bucket that hung in the well."

On questions of public policy the pioneer had decided opinions. His New England or New York education had fixed these firm and unchangeable, and the partisans of Jackson and Clay, Van Buren and Harrison argued their respective merits and demerits, as warmly as we do to-day. But office-seekers were scarce and office-holders scarcer, though they existed then, as now, a sort of necessary evil.

One of the most prominent characteristics of the old time was the universal hospitality and helpfulness that abounded everywhere. The latch string ran through the door. The belated traveler was sure of rest at the first house. Everybody was ready to help in case of accident to wagon or cattle. "Lend a hand" was the motto of the pioneer. Teams were hitched together for breaking up; in harvest time the neighbors cradled and raked and bound for one another; when one went to mill, he went for the neighborhood; logging bees and husking bees, quilting bees and raisings were play-spells. We boast, and very justly too, of all that machinery has done for us, and especially in the field of agriculture; but has it ever occurred to you how much it has done to make machines of us? We have no need to call upon our neighbor for help in the harvest field—the reaper takes his place. The old fashioned quilting, with its gossip and talk, its evening frolic and games, has departed. The sewing machine does the work of willing hands in the long ago. We are not as dependent or as generous in these days as in the old ones. We ask less, and of course give less.

We are richer and the world is richer for its inventions, though I cannot help thinking that the swelling of our pocket-books is accompanied by a shrinking of our hearts. Whether this be so or not, the hospitality, the generosity, the helping hand and kindly heart that made "the world akin" when we were young, are worth remembering and imitating as we grow old.

The pioneer was a worker.

"From toil he wins his spirits light,
From busy day the peaceful night;
Rich, from the very want of wealth,
In heaven's best treasures—peace and health."

I don't know that he loved work any better than we do, but he had to do it, and every body around him, wife and children, worked to. "God and the angels were the only lookers-on" in the old time.

The boys held the plough and the girls held the baby. The wife rocked the cradle and ran the spinning wheel at the same time, and to the same tune. To get the trees out and the crops in was the ambition of the family, and they all helped.

When I hear a farmer, who has cleared up his farm, built his buildings, planted his orchards, and is out of debt, all from the sweat of his own brow, say "I have done my share, I mean to sit on the fence and see somebody else work hereafter," I honor him for the good work of his younger days and for the good sense of his latter ones, and devoutly say, amen. Now I confess I don't like hard work, and presume you don't; yet in these times of depression and financial distress, when statesmen or men who think they are statesmen, financiers, and political economists are groping in the dark for some measures of relief, proposing all sorts of impossible schemes, legislating this way and that—calling a dollar two dollars if you owe a debt, and fifty cents if somebody owes you—imagining that an act of Congress may prove a magician's wand by which hard times may be waved away and good times beckoned in, I sometimes think that the only path that will lead us back to prosperity is the highway of labor, productive industry, old fashioned hard work, that will enable us to produce more than we consume, earn more than we spend and export more than we import.

Too many of us are trying to get a living without work, by trading in something—operating, as it is called in fashionable commercial circles—or in some way that is comfortable and easy and, as we think, respectable.

I do not wonder at this; it is natural and I see no blame in it, but it is not healthful. None of us want our boys to have quite as hard a time as we had when we were boys, (I know I don't for one), the boy's heart that still beats under our vest says this, but as plain, practical men I am not sure but we do our boys an injury in this feeling.

At all events we should hold up to them the idea that the law of labor is the law of humanity, that work is honorable, dignified and profitable, and the sort of stuff that men are made of.

A world without heroes would indeed be a poor one. We in America have had our full share, and in this year of all others we love to talk of them. Heroes of every generation are the common legacy of our citizenship, and how fondly, yet boastingly, we recall the names on the long roll of honor; with what honest pride we recount the heroic acts that adorn every page of our history; with what tender remembrance have we embalmed in our memories the actors.

"Their swords are rust,
Their bones are dust,
Their souls are with the saints we trust."

When we remember Michigan as it was forty years ago, and see it as it is to-day, we realize that "Peace hath her victories no less renowned than war," and that we too have our heroes, whose laurels have been gained in the paths of peace—conquerors not of their fellow men but of nature itself.

The man who steps on to a forty or eighty acre lot of wild land with only his ax for a helper, and says "Here is to be my home—here me and mine shall, by-and-by, sit under the shade of our own vine and tree—here shall be rest and peace and quiet content"—is indeed a hero.

His banner is always a flag of truce, his trophies the fallen tree and burning log-heap, his reward, the prosperity and happiness, that blesses us to-day. In his work the wife and mother have done their share, and if we christen him a hero, we must not forget that they are heroines, enduring privation without complaint, rearing the family in the fear of God and to habits of industry, helping neighbor and stranger alike, foremost in school and church work, with a kindly greeting for tired husband or boy, with good words for the faint-hearted beginner, or weary new-comer; have they not earned our adoration, are they not heroines indeed?

The one grand impelling power that directed the pioneer was the idea of *home*. He left the home of his boyhood, not to float idly on the world's surface, not to tarry here a while and there a while, but with the fixed, firm purpose of founding a home of his own. He knew that states and communities, cities and villages would follow his footsteps, but the goal he strove for was home. For him, "East or West, home's best." The love of home we bear to-day is our inheritance from the fathers, "more to be desired than gold, yea, than much fine gold, sweeter also than honey and the honey comb." Let us cherish it, increase it with watchful care, and as new swarms go out from the parent hive, let them settle in hives of their own, remembering that

"There is a spot of earth supremely blest,
A dearer, sweeter spot than all the rest,
Where man, creation's tyrant, casts aside
His sword and sceptre, pageantry and pride,
While in his looks benignly blend
The sire, the son, husband, brother, friend;
Here woman reigns, the mother, daughter, wife,
Strew with fresh flowers, the narrow way of life!
In the clear heaven of her delightful eye,
An angel-guard of love and graces lie;
Around her knees domestic duties meet,
And fireside pleasures gambol at her feet.
Where shall that land, that spot of earth be found?
Art thou a man?—a patriot—look around:
O, thou shalt find, however thy footsteps roam,
That land *thy* country, and that spot *thy* home."

The spirit of unrest, of conquest, and of progress that has animated the Anglo-Saxon for so many centuries is the spirit of pioneership. The men and women of the May-flower, when they cast anchor in Plymouth Bay, saw in the land that gladdened their eyes a home free from persecution, a land where they could worship God with freedom and in accordance with the dictates of their own conscience, and that was all. They knew not that the hand that guided them in the pursuit of religious freedom had chosen them as the founders of a nation. They felt not the power of the spirit of civilization impelling them.

They did not realize that in the wake of their craft, there followed the steamship, the locomotive and the telegraph. In the little cabin of that vessel the arts and sciences, invention and discovery, commerce and trade were unseen passengers.

At its masthead floated the simple banner of the cross, and though the red, white and blue of the December sky hung over them, they did not see in it the flag of a nation of forty millions of people.

All this they knew not, for in the small compass of their ken they only saw the immediate present. They forgot that the blood of the centuries that flowed in their veins was that of the pioneer.

Our own pioneers—and we too—have not recognized this in our rovings and migrations. They, and we set out on our pilgrimage to find a home for ourselves, and have established empires and builded States. The divine purposes of the Great Ruler have been entrusted to the pioneer. He has been the instrument in subduing the waste places, in civilizing and humanizing the world. The pathway he carved out has become the highway upon which the world is traveling, bearing in its train the civilization of the nineteenth century—laden with the love of liberty and freedom—freighted with the noblest, highest hopes of humanity. The great procession is still in motion; it cannot pause or stop; still there are worlds to conquer—still there is work for the pioneer.

The Pilgrim Fathers founded the nation, their sons saved it and it is ours to preserve and perpetuate. Let us then, in this birthyear, highly resolve to be true to the blood of the pilgrim and the pioneer that courses through our veins. They laid the foundation strong and sure; it is for us to complete the structure. Let us see to it then that our work be well done, so that with us, education and morality, religion and liberty, free thought and free speech shall abide forever.

"For the structure that we raise,
Time is with materials filled;
Our to-days and yesterdays
Are the blocks with which we build.

Truly shape and fashion these,
Leave no yawning gaps between;
Think not, because no man sees
Such things will remain unseen.

Thus alone can we attain
To those turrets, where the eye
Sees the world as one vast plain,
And one boundless reach of sky."

www.ingramcontent.com/pod-product-compliance
Lightning Source LLC
LaVergne TN
LVHW020641110826
845149LV00004B/1310

* 9 7 8 1 4 1 8 1 8 9 8 0 8 *